Thirty Days

A DEVOTIONAL

through

COLOSSIANS

A DEVOTIONAL
through
COLOSSIANS

MIKE MACINTOSH

✦ HORIZON**PRESS**™ / San Diego, CA

Published in San Diego, California by Horizon Press, P.O. Box 17480, San Diego, California 92177.

All Scripture quotations, unless otherwise noted, are taken from the New King James Version (NKJV) Copyright © 1982 by Thomas Nelson, Inc. Used by permission. All rights reserved.

Library of Congress Cataloging-in-Publication Data available upon request.

Printed in the United States of America

ISBN-13/EAN: 978-1-60412-009-7

07 08 09 10 11 12   9 8 7 6 5 4 3 2 1

Contents

Introduction

Have you ever taken the time to consider the fact that when you're reading Paul's writings in the New Testament, you're essentially reading someone's mail? Each of his epistles—including the book of Colossians—is a letter. The apostle wrote them with beloved people in mind, and they carried a message he wanted them to hear. Paul's heart longed to see believers drawing closer to God, walking with Him each day, and growing in their faith.

This devotional bears with it an invitation to open up the envelope with Colosse's postmark and unfold the pages found within. Paul has a message for us—one that points to what God has in store. For the next thirty days, we'll be walking through each chapter and verse of the wonderful, powerful, practical Book of Colossians. May this devotional unfold God's Word in a fresh way and touch you with His message.

 Day 1

GRACE AND PEACE

Paul, an apostle of Jesus Christ by the will of God, and Timothy our brother, to the saints and faithful brethren in Christ who are in Colosse: Grace to you and peace from God our Father and the Lord Jesus Christ.

—Colossians 1:1-2

Grace and peace have been referred to as the inseparable twins of the New Testament. In just about every book of the New Testament, the introduction begins with *grace* and *peace*. In every case, grace comes first, followed by peace. Our lives follow this model; without experiencing the grace of God, you do not experience the peace of God.

If you are looking for peace in your life today, you will never find it unless you first find God's grace. The only way to get that peace is to know God's grace. And the grace of God is His unmerited favor toward you. You don't deserve it, and you can't earn it, but it is available to you today simply because *He loves you.*

Those of us that lived during the 1960's remember the peace sign and people saying, "Peace, man." It is ironic that with everyone talking about peace, hippies were the most messed up generation ever, and what they were lacking most was *peace.*

So many people thought that drugs and alcohol brought peace, but they didn't. They made us high and low, up and down, crash and burn. We had a fake peace for a little while, but even that ended once the drugs and alcohol wore off. And the search for even fake peace continues to this generation.

The only real, true source of peace is from God. He is our perfect peace. Jesus promised us a peace that passes all understanding (Philippians 4:7), and that is what you need when you are hurting, when you are troubled, and when you are discouraged. You don't need a pretend peace that will alter with your emotions, your circumstances, or your relationships temporarily; you need unwavering peace that is based on the Word.

Today, if you are not experiencing the peace of God, you are probably not experiencing the grace of God. If that is you, simply accept God's love and forgiveness. And from this moment on, go with grace and peace.

Day 2

- -

HOPE OF HEAVEN

- -

*We give thanks to the God and Father of our Lord
Jesus Christ, praying always for you, since we heard
of your faith in Christ Jesus and of your love for all the
saints; because of the hope which is laid up for you in
Heaven, of which you heard before in the word of the
truth of the gospel, which has come to you, as it has
also in all the world, and is bringing forth fruit, as it
is also among you since the day you heard and knew
the grace of God in truth; as you also learned from
Epaphras, our dear fellow servant, who is a faithful
minister of Christ on your behalf, who also declared to
us your love in the Spirit.*

—Colossians 1:3-8

There are two very practical points that I would like to draw your attention to from Paul's introduction. The first point is that Paul wanted the Colossians to know that he prayed for them all of the time. Paul had tremendous love for the body of Christ and demonstrated that love by praying for them. One of the best things we can ever do for anyone is to pray for them. Additionally, I have found that when I pray for other people, it causes me to take my eyes off of myself and things concerning me, and gets me focused on other people and their needs.

The second point that Paul makes is that our hope is laid up for us in Heaven. What an interesting thought. There is something outside of the realm in which we currently live. By putting your faith in Jesus Christ as your Lord and Savior, you have hope! And once we, as Christians, break out of this realm, whether by death or by rapture, we enter into something that is so wonderful!

As Christians, our ultimate hope is spending eternity with Jesus in Heaven, but until then we have the amazing opportunity and privilege to pray while we are here on earth; for our family, our friends, our church, missionaries, government officials, and the list goes on. May we find ourselves praying for others more and more until that day when we enter into Heaven—our ultimate hope.

Day 3

WALKING WORTHY

For this reason we also, since the day we heard it, do not cease to pray for you, and to ask that you may be filled with the knowledge of His will in all wisdom and spiritual understanding; that you may walk worthy of the Lord, fully pleasing Him, being fruitful in every good work and increasing in the knowledge of God; strengthened with all might, according to His glorious power, for all patience and longsuffering with joy.

—Colossians 1:9-11

Walking worthy of the Lord is something I desire to do with all of my heart, which means I want to be filled with His will, all wisdom, spiritual understanding, and fully pleasing Him. I get very upset with myself if I have done something or said something that would displease the Lord. Before I was born again, I was in control of my life and it was a mess. But since surrendering my heart and life to Jesus, my life has been a blessing and I am dedicated to try and please the Lord. I want my whole life to be for Him and not for me.

As you read this, perhaps you are wondering how in the world can you walk worthy of the Lord, or be fully pleasing to Him? After all, you can get frustrated with the kids, or disappointed by your spouse; you are not perfect.

But read again in today's passage: *according to His glorious power.* As we walk in God's grace and yield our lives over to the power and working of the Holy Spirit, He enables us to walk worthy, to please Him, to be fruitful, to increase in knowledge, and to be strengthened with all might. These are things we cannot do for ourselves in our own strength, because they are of the Holy Spirit. As we surrender and die daily to ourselves, we allow His grace, power, and Spirit to work in our lives on a continual basis.

Day 4

- -

THE JOY OF THE LORD

- -

...strengthened with all might, according to His glorious power, for all patience and longsuffering with joy;

—Colossians 1:11

Like the peace of God, the joy of the Lord is something that by God's grace is available to every believer, whether rich or poor, healthy or ill, young or old.

> *The joy of the Lord is your strength.*
> —*Nehemiah 8:10*

> *And these things we write to you that your joy may be full.*
> —*1 John 1:4*

Are you experiencing joy in your walk with Jesus? Let's look at the words of Paul as he addresses the Colossians and draw some application that will help you to experience the joy of the Lord. If you believe the fact that God loves, accepts, and forgives you, you will begin to experience the grace and peace of God.

First, you will most likely start praying for other people. This will help you take your eyes off yourself and your own issues, and bless you in ways beyond all you could ask or think! Next, you will be strengthened with might because you know His Word and the hope of Heaven.

Joy is something we receive from the Lord Himself, who never changes. Therefore, it is possible to be strengthened with the joy of the Lord, regardless of our circumstances. We may not be physically feeling well, but we can always experience joy. I may have had a tough day with the kids, but by God's grace and His Holy Spirit, I still have joy; joy that I am His child, joy that my sins are forgiven, joy that I am headed to Heaven.

But until we get to Heaven, we can be His vessels of love here on earth, *strengthened with all might, according to His glorious power, for all patience and longsuffering with joy.*

 S

- -

QUALIFIED

- -

Giving thanks to the Father who has qualified us to be
partakers of the inheritance of the saints in the light.

—*Colossians 1:12*

The word *qualified* in today's passage is quite an important word. Vine's Dictionary tells us this word means to "render fit" or "make sufficient." You see, as Christians, our Heavenly Father has made us sufficient to receive the inheritance of the saints in the light. We are qualified for Heaven, not because of anything we have done or can do, but because God Himself has done the work of making us perfectly fit.

As a chaplain for the San Diego Police Department, I have an electronic card that enables me to enter the police station parking lot and through the door where the police officers enter and exit. I have been qualified to go into restricted areas. People that have not been qualified cannot go where I can.

In a similar manner, God has qualified His children for access into the Kingdom of Light. As adopted heirs, we are made sufficient, we are rendered fit, and we are qualified to enter God's Kingdom. Those who are not saved and born again are not qualified (yet) to partake of His inheritance. By the blood of Jesus, we who accept Him as Lord and Saviour are partakers of the inheritance. It's no wonder that Paul starts this statement by giving thanks.

Why not take some time today and let your Father know how thankful you are for His willingness to qualify you for Heaven?

Day 6

- -

THE KINGDOM OF HIS LOVE AND LIGHT

- -

He has delivered us from the power of darkness and
conveyed us into the kingdom of the Son of His love.
—Colossians 1:13

The word *conveyed* refers to land being transferred to a king who has just conquered an entire empire. The property now belongs to the conquering king and his kingdom. Other translations use the words, *translated* or *transferred,* which are all very good to describe the very powerful for for us today.

You see, before you were a Christian, the power of darkness held you. But by the blood of Jesus, He conquered the darkness; transferring, translating, and conveying you into the light. With the love of Jesus, He transferred you into the kingdom of His love. As Christians, we are no longer under the control of darkness; we no longer live in that kingdom. Darkness has been conquered and we live with Jesus in the light.

And as we walk in the light, just as the moon reflects the light of the sun, we too are to reflect the light of the Son —Jesus—to our friends, to our families, to our co-workers, and to everyone we meet. They can experience that same conquering love that you and I have experienced, and be transferred, translated, and conveyed into the Kingdom of Light.

Day 7

REDEMPTION

...in whom [Jesus] we have redemption through His blood, the forgiveness of sins.

—Colossians 1:14

Redemption is not a word that most people use in their everyday conversations, but it is a very powerful word that can change your life in an instant. You see, to be redeemed means that you have been set free or have been ransomed in full. It carries the idea of an enslaved person being set free, released, no longer a slave.

For the person who has not yet received Jesus as Savior, they are a slave to sin and still in darkness under the control of the devil. But once you confess with your mouth the Lord Jesus and believe in your heart that God has raised Him from the dead (Romans 10:9), you are at that very moment redeemed. The blood of Jesus has paid the price; you have been ransomed and set free.

God loves you so much that He sent Jesus, His only begotten Son to die on a cross for you so that you would be transferred in to His Kingdom and redeemed, set free from the sin and bondage that once entangled you.

Are you walking like a person who has been set free? Are you still chained down by the lust of the flesh, the lust of the eyes, or the pride of life? Don't listen to the lies of the devil. Listen to God through reading His Word. Yes, you once were a prisoner, but Jesus has ransomed you by His blood—you are free!

> *But if we walk in the light as He is in the light, we have fellowship with one another, and the blood of Jesus Christ His Son cleanses us from all sin.*
> —*1 John 1:7*

May the Holy Spirit help each one of us to walk in the Light as He is in the Light.

Day 8

- -

FULLY GOD

- -

For it pleased the Father that in Him all the fullness should dwell, and by Him to reconcile all things to Himself, by Him, whether things on earth or things in Heaven, having made peace through the blood of His cross.

—Colossians 1:19-20

There are two words that I would like to draw your attention to as we look at this amazing verse. The first is the word *dwell*, which literally means, "to be at home permanently." And the second word is *fullness*, which was a word that the Gnostic teachers of Paul's day used to describe the sum total of all divine power and attributes.

The Gnostics did not believe that Jesus could be God because he was also a physical being. They did not believe that a human could also be Divine because human beings are made of the flesh; they did not believe that anyone born into a body of flesh could be perfect. This is why Paul chose the words he did. Paul was telling the people, the Gnostics in particular, that Jesus *permanently houses all divine power and authority.*

> *For in Him dwells all the fullness of the Godhead bodily.*
> —*Colossians 2:9*

You see, it pleased our Heavenly Father to place within Jesus every bit of power and authority. This is such an important concept for us to grasp. Jesus was not part God and part man. No, although in a human/physical body, the entire *fullness* of the Godhead *dwelt* (permanently resided) within Him. He was fully God. And as God, He alone was able to reconcile sinful man to a perfect and holy God.

Today is the day to make things right with God—to ask His forgiveness, believe His promises, and be reconciled to Him. When the day comes that you stand before God (whether through death or Rapture), Jesus will present *you* to the Father as holy.

Day 9

AT PEACE

And you, who once were alienated and enemies in your
mind by wicked works, yet now He has reconciled in
the body of His flesh through death, to present you
holy, and blameless, and above reproach in His sight.
—Colossians 1:21-22

What an amazing thought that you and I, who at one time were at war with God, hating the things of God by our wicked works, alienated and enemies of Him, can get to the place where we are at peace with God. Our Lord Jesus Christ is the only One who can change you from being a person at war with God to a person who is a friend of God.

By His precious blood that was poured out on the cross we are reconciled to Him and, therefore, at peace. Apart from the blood of Jesus, no one can be reconciled to God. He paid the price and we are free. We are no longer at war with God, but we are at peace with God through the blood of His cross.

Is that wonderful or what? Once alienated, now reconciled. At one point in time you were one thing, but now you are something different; you are no longer what you were. For the Christian, your standing before the Lord is reconciled. There is no longer anything separating you from God. Please notice that the word *reconciled* is past tense—it has already happened, and there is nothing more that needs to be done for you to be reconciled to God.

> *Therefore, if anyone is in Christ, he is a new creation; old things have passed away; behold, all things have become new.*
> —*2 Corinthians 5:17*

The old you is gone. If you belong to Jesus, you are a new creation and the old things have passed away—not "are passing" or "will pass," but they have already passed away—past tense.

> *From the bottom of our hearts, we thank you, God, for the tremendous price You paid to reconcile us to Yourself; we cannot thank You enough. I would like to pray for every man and woman, boy and girl, reading this, that they would receive a tender touch from You. In Jesus name, Amen.*

Day 40

- -

HIS PLANS AND PURPOSES

- -

To them God willed to make known what are the riches of the glory of this mystery among the Gentiles: which is Christ in you, the hope of glory.

—Colossians 1:27

The last few words of this verse are words that every Christian should know: *Christ in you, the hope of glory.* I can remember many years ago hearing a great man of God, Major Ian Thomas. He had an amazing gift of explaining this whole concept of *Christ in us,* which I appreciated as I began to mature in my walk with Jesus. I began to understand that with Christ in me, I was to be a vehicle that God could use to touch the lives of others. Because Jesus is inside of me, He can use my hands to help others. He can use my heart to have compassion and mercy. And the more that I die to myself, the more Jesus can use me for His plans and purposes.

And because Jesus is in you, you have the hope of glory. Going to Heaven is not based on your tithing or your attendance at prayer meetings. It is based on Jesus Christ; His death on the cross, His resurrection from the dead, and receiving Him into your heart. And because I have this hope, I want to be a vehicle that God can use to share His love with others. May God use each of us to be a vehicle that brings the love of Jesus to a dying world.

Day 11

RICHES AND TREASURES

For I want you to know what a great conflict I have for
you and those in Laodicea, and for as many as have
not seen my face in the flesh, that their hearts may be
encouraged, being knit together in love, and attaining
to all riches of the full assurance of understanding,
to the knowledge of the mystery of God, both of the
Father and of Christ, in whom are hidden all the
treasures of wisdom and knowledge.

—*Colossians 2:1-3*

We live in a world that doesn't want us to go to the pages of Scripture to find true wisdom. This world does not want us to look up. Rather, it wants us to look around to people and the society for answers and advice.

It's nothing new; Paul recognized this problem in his day, too. Paul had a deep love for the church and a desire to see the Christians at Colosse come to a rich, full understanding of God and Jesus Christ. His passionate and encouraging counsel for the church was to be knit together in love and attain the riches of understanding and knowledge of the mystery of God. Today, as we start this second chapter of Colossians, his encouragements are very relevant for us as well.

Another way to consider that something is knit together is to understand that it is joined, interlaced, bound, and united. This kind of relationship is how we relate to our Lord. Paul first beseeches the church body to be woven together. Being spiritually likeminded and loving God and one another is our first call as a Christian.

Are you interested in becoming rich? In God's economy, it is simple. It's not striving in your career to make money or watch the stocks or invest in bigger and better real estate deals. The richness in God's economy is the full assurance of understanding the knowledge of the mystery of God, which is both the Father and the Son. The hidden treasures of wisdom and knowledge are found in the Bible, and the treasure map is in every book, chapter, and verse.

May you prosper as you follow the Biblical map to find the riches and treasure of wisdom and knowledge.

Day 12

WISDOM ELIMINATES DECEPTION

Now this I say lest anyone should deceive you with persuasive words. For though I am absent in the flesh, yet I am with you in spirit, rejoicing to see your good order and the steadfastness of your faith in Christ.

—Colossians 2:4-5

Paul warns us to beware of being deceived by persuasive words. We live in a world where persuasive words are coming at us all the time. Whether the words are coming from marketing companies trying to get us to buy a product, or another religion coming to our door, people are constantly trying to persuade us to think and believe their artificial rhetoric.

Back in the 1960's, I went to a home in Beverly Hills where Maharishi Mahesh Yogi was staying. I went there because the Maharishi persuaded me that I could find peace in my life by practicing transcendental meditation. But I soon discovered that was a lie, I was deceived, and I did not have peace. *Religions* can only take you so far spiritually.

Paul was writing to the church at Colosse from Rome; he was not there among the people. But the Holy Spirit is among us. Like Paul, He rejoices in seeing our good order and steadfastness in our faith in Christ, not in lip-service by people trying to persuade and deceive you who do not have any accountability to the Lord. So what they say is irrelevant. Keep your eyes upon Jesus, look full in His wonderful face. As He said in John 14:6:

> *I am the way, the truth, and the life. No one comes to the Father except through Me.*

Day 13

ESTABLISHED IN JESUS

As you therefore have received Christ Jesus the
Lord, so walk in Him, rooted and built up in Him
and established in the faith, as you have been taught,
abounding in it with thanksgiving.

—*Colossians 2:6-7*

We can all get overwhelmed by the difficulties of life, but we need to be reminded during stressful times that God has specific purposes and plans for our lives; they are not plans to hurt or harm us, but rather to root us, and build us up, in Jesus Christ. You and I are just like clay on a potter's wheel, and it is God who has put us on the wheel, where His hands are molding and shaping our lives:

> *The word which came to Jeremiah from the LORD,*
> *saying: "Arise and go down to the potter's house, and*
> *there I will cause you to hear My words." Then I went*
> *down to the potter's house, and there he was, making*
> *something at the wheel. And the vessel that he made of*

clay was marred in the hand of the potter; so he made
it again into another vessel, as it seemed good to the
potter to make. Then the word of the LORD came to
me, saying: "O house of Israel, can I not do with you
as this potter?" says the LORD. "Look, as the clay is
in the potter's hand, so are you in My hand, O house
of Israel!"

—Jeremiah 18:1-6

You see, God brought Jeremiah to the potter's house to illustrate how He has His shaping hands on each one of our lives this very moment. Some of you, however, may be trying to jump off the wheel and run away from God because the substantial shaping and molding from His hands are too uncomfortable.

And we know that all things work together for good
to those who love God, to those who are the called
according to His purpose.

—Romans 8:28

This verse is a promise, an assurance, and an encouragement. It doesn't start with "And we feel..." or any other uncertainty. It starts with "And *we know*..." We can be confident that this passage is proven and genuine! And notice that it doesn't say *some* things work together for good. And it doesn't say all things will be easy. It does say *all things* work together for *good*.

I don't have all of the answers and I don't know why some things are happening to you, but I do know that one day (though it may be many years down the road), the picture will become clear, and you will understand why you are going through the trials you face today. Friends, whatever you are going through today, remember that it is happening so that you will be built up in Jesus—molded and shaped by your loving Father's hands.

Day 14

SEARCH THE SCRIPTURES DAILY

----

*Beware lest anyone cheat you through philosophy
and empty deceit, according to the tradition of men,
according to the basic principles of the world, and not
according to Christ.*

—*Colossians 2:8*

Paul warns us to beware that we are not cheated through philosophy and empty deceit according to the traditions of men. Remember, Paul was writing this to the Gnostics who primarily based their teachings on worldly tradition. I know there have been some great philosophers through the centuries; deep thinkers with inspiring ideas. But consider when those ideas are devoid of God, as in the philosophy of Paul's day—they may be interesting ideas, but they are ultimately empty. Paul understood Proverbs 9:10: "the fear of the Lord is the beginning of wisdom," and so he warned us not to be tricked by the writings and traditions of men into a fruitless pursuit of wisdom and knowledge.

May I encourage you to search the Scriptures daily, to seek wisdom from His Word. All of the influences around us that are constantly trying to persuade us to think and act inconsistently towards the things of the Lord are sometimes overwhelming. By searching the Scriptures daily, you will be filled with Godly wisdom and knowledge.

Day 45

COMPLETE IN HIM

For in Him dwells all the fullness of the Godhead
bodily; and you are complete in Him, who is the head of
all principality and power.
                                        —Colossians 2:9-10

I love the book of Colossians because it speaks so clearly about the preeminence of Jesus Christ, and gives us so much practical help for living the Christian life. We learn that we don't have to *work* at being a Christian. The result of having the Holy Spirit in your life is that He enables you to die to those things that are self-serving, which allows more of Jesus to shine through your life.

We have all experienced trials or tribulations that bring hurt and heartache, but God allows these things to come into our lives to cause our flesh to die, and to pave the way for the Holy Spirit to shape us into men and women who are ready for Heaven. Now for most of us, we would prefer *the easy road* or the proverbial *bed of roses,* but that is seldom the way God builds character into our lives.

How we respond to the trials and tribulations is our choice; we can respond positively, trusting that the Lord is going to accomplish something wonderful, or we can respond negatively, questioning why God would allow this to happen. As you allow the Lord Jesus to be preeminent in your heart and life, when you go through trials and tribulations, you will find that by the power of the Holy Spirit you will have greater trust—and even joy—as you are being shaped into that man or woman who is ready for Heaven.

Day 16

ALIVE AND FORGIVEN

He has made alive together with Him, having forgiven
you all trespasses, having wiped out the handwriting
of requirements that was against us, which was
contrary to us. And He has taken it out of the way,
having nailed it to the cross.

—Colossians 2:13b-14

He is alive! And He has the power to make us alive with Him. Life is so precious. Life with Him is glorious. Is there a song in your heart and a skip in your step? Do you smile at others? Do you talk about Jesus, your Savior, the Love of your life? Are you encouraging to those at work or school who are down, even though you barely know them? Do you share your talents that God has given you and give the offering back to Him, glorifying His Holy Name? If you answer yes to any of these questions, then be thankful. These are some ways that He has made you alive.

We were dead in our sins, but once He forgave us we started living again. We were forgiven all of our trespasses. The word *all* means *all*. Any sin—in God's eyes, little sins and big sins are all the same. He wants to forgive us, but we need to come to Him and ask for forgiveness first. It's a joy for Him to forgive us. He wants us in Heaven with Him for eternity. He wants to wipe out the handwriting of requirements against us. Those things can be in your past today, forever, if you just give them to Him and leave them at the foot of the cross.

He will take it out of the way and leave it there—nailed to the cross. Surrender to Him, completely; pour out all of your heart, soul, mind, and strength to Him. His power is greater than you can even begin to imagine. He holds the universe in the span of His hand, and the oceans in the hollow of His hand. The Heavens were made for Him, as they expand and become more beautiful and fascinating. As high as the Heaven, so is His love for you, and you cannot even imagine Heaven's highest point, because it is growing ever higher. That's how His love is for you. He loves you abundantly more than you could ever ask or think.

Think on these things.

Day 17

THE CROSS OF FREEDOM

Therefore, if you died with Christ from the basic
principles of the world, why, as though living in the
world, do you subject yourselves to regulations—"Do
not touch, do not taste, do not handle," which all
concern things which perish with the using—according
to the commandments and doctrines of men? These
things indeed have an appearance of wisdom in self-
imposed religion, false humility, and neglect of the
body, but are of no value against the indulgence of the
flesh.

—Colossians 2:20-23

Jesus did not die on a cross for you to be bound by rules and regulations. In this passage from Colossians 2, Paul continues to warn the church against self-imposed religion and false humility, two things that demean and distort the simple truth of the Gospel.

False humility and religion say, "If I don't touch this or eat that, if I pray often enough or do enough good things, then I can be righteous and pleasing to God." But that does not follow the teaching of Jesus. It was not Jesus or the Bible that taught the people not to touch, taste, or handle; it was the doctrines of men. Men wanted to look holy and righteous outwardly, and this is exactly what Paul is warning against.

Rules and regulations do not make us righteous—only the redeeming blood of Jesus can do that. Be assured that Jesus died on a cross for you—in order to wipe out the handwriting of requirements that were against you; they have been nailed to the cross.

> *...having wiped out the handwriting of requirements that was against us, which was contrary to us. And He has taken it out of the way, having nailed it to the cross.*
>
> *—Colossians 2:14*

You are set free!

Day 48

HEAVENLY MINDED

If then you were raised with Christ, seek those things which are above, where Christ is, sitting at the right hand of God.

—*Colossians 3:1*

There sure are a lot of *ifs* in our lives. And those *ifs* point to the existence of things in our lives that are unsettled, undecided upon. Over the years, I have met so many people who live in the land of *if* and *maybe*—they are unsettled and unsure. But the word *if* has nothing to do with uncertainty here in the third chapter of Colossians. In the Greek language of Paul's day, it could actually be translated, "since it is already settled and established."

As Christians, our eternity is *already settled and established.* Our home is being prepared. And while we are waiting, the Holy Spirit is preparing *us* for Heaven. That's why Paul instructs us to seek those things, and set our minds on the things, which are above. As we do, we will find ourselves living in the place of assurance and trust with Him.

> *The LORD will perfect that which concerns me.*
> —*Psalm 138:8a*

Take a minute and think about your relationship with Jesus and your pursuit of the things of God. Would you use the words *urgency* or *strong desire* to describe your pursuit of the things of God? Those are the words Paul has in mind when he tells us to seek those things which are above. Paul is telling us that since we were raised with Christ, we must, with an urgency and desire, seek the things that are above. Seeking the things that are above is not to be a casual, easy-going thing we just happen to do. No, we need to pour ourselves into it.

When we watch the Olympic Games, we see people competing in athletic events with a sense of urgency, with a strong desire to win so that they can have a gold medal hung around their neck. Imagine if you and I had that same urgency and desire to seek the things that are above, and to supernaturally allow His Holy Spirit to use us to be His agents—His vessels—to touch the hearts and lives of the people around us.

Lord, we thank you that You, by the power of Your Holy Spirit, that You give us opportunities to grow and change. It is so easy to seek pleasure, financial gain, and things that are not good for us. But today, we are asking that You would help us to seek those things which are above, with a sense of urgency, knowing that You are coming back very soon. We ask Your help today, that we would allow You to have more control in our hearts and lives than ever before. In the name of Jesus Christ, Your Son, Amen.

Day 19

THINGS ABOVE

Set your mind on things above, not on things on the earth.

—Colossians 3:2

It is true that if you set your mind on the things of this world, you will probably accomplish those things. In the business community, there are plenty of opportunities to climb to the top of the corporate ladder if you are willing to sacrifice all of your time, your family, your health, and possibly your ethics, morals, and ultimately the Lord. Additionally, athletes have opportunities to participate in the Olympic Games, baseball, football, tennis, etc., but they also sacrifice many of the same things that those in the business community would have to forsake.

But I have yet to find anybody at their deathbed, in all the years I have done funerals, or stood by people dying on the highway or from gunshot wounds at the hospital, that has told me how important their possessions were to them.

Is it wrong to seek things that are in this world? Is it wrong to want a nice house or new clothes? I don't believe those things are wrong in and of themselves. But what motivates our desires for those things? Do we believe that acquiring certain "things" will make us look more important, solve our problems, or cause us to feel better about ourselves? I believe the problem is when "things" start taking control of us—when we rely on them to fulfill and define us—they become our life.

What if we turn our desires over to the Lord for Him to be glorified in the house we live in, the car we drive, or the clothes we wear? Consider how we can be a witness in all circumstances, through our possessions. Imagine finding a dream home, one that you can afford, but there's a waiting period for His answer as to whether or not you should buy it. Can you offer it to the Lord? Can you tell Him that it's truly up to Him whether you are to live there or not? What can be done with the dream home if He says "yes," that will glorify him? During every phase of the offer, buying, financing, and decorating, can we give Him the glory? Can we use it only and primarily for His purposes? And, what if He says "no" after the waiting period? Can we also offer that up to Him? Be thankful in everything!

When you are seeking the things of God and you are setting your mind on Jesus, *He becomes your life*. He fulfills you; He gives you guidance and direction. And the Holy Spirit empowers you to discern right from wrong, important from unimportant.

I don't know what you are seeking or setting your mind on today, but I do know that if you will do what Paul is instructing you to do, your life will radically change from this very minute.

Day 20

CHRIST OUR LIFE

For you died, and your life is hidden with Christ in God. When Christ who is our life appears, then you also will appear with Him in glory.

—Colossians 3:3-4

Listen to how Paul describes his relationship with Jesus: "When Christ, *who is our life...*" Paul gives to Jesus one of the greatest titles of devotion; he calls Him the *Christ of our life.* And when Jesus is your life, He will overflow it and make you into the man or woman He wants you to be.

What is your life wrapped up in today? Some people have their lives hidden in a bottle of beer; others have their lives hidden in the size of their stock portfolio or bank account, while still others have their lives hidden behind the local gang.

When I was growing up as a kid, I didn't live in the best of neighborhoods and there were some rough guys in gangs that liked to fight and cause trouble. And as a kid, I was either fighting my way out, lying my way out, or manipulating my way out of situations on a regular basis. But when I learned that I could be hidden in Christ, and that He protects and directs me, boy that sure took a load off of me.

When our lives are hidden in Christ and we allow Him to have the preeminence in our lives, we won't have to lie, we won't have to fight, we won't be depending on the bottle or our finances for our strength—we will be relying on Jesus Christ to bring us through each minute, each hour, and each day, all the way up until the time He comes back to take us up into Heaven.

Take inventory today. Is your life hidden in Christ? Would you describe Jesus as your life, or are other things crowding Him out? Jesus loves you so much. Don't look to or rely on anything else but Him!

Day 21

- -

DEATH TO SIN

- -

Therefore put to death your members which are on the earth: fornication, uncleanness, passion, evil desire, and covetousness, which is idolatry. Because of these things the wrath of God is coming upon the sons of disobedience, in which you yourselves once walked when you lived in them.

—Colossians 3:5-7

When we, as Believers, get to Heaven, we will not struggle with sin. But until that day, we are here on earth and Paul reminds us that those sins that keep us from God are to be put to death. We are not told to hide our sins or try and cover them up; we are told to put the old man (Romans 6:11) to death so that the old sinful nature would not have any control over us.

As we look at the world around us, we see that the power of sin is very strong. And if we will be honest with ourselves, we also recognize that the temptation to sin is strong. But the good news for the disciple of Jesus is that we don't have to give in to sin.

> *I have been crucified with Christ; it is no longer I who live, but Christ lives in me; and the life which I now live in the flesh I live by faith in the Son of God, who loved me and gave Himself for me.*
>
> *—Galatians 2:20*

> *Therefore, brethren, we are debtors—not to the flesh, to live according to the flesh. For if you live according to the flesh you will die; but if by the Spirit you put to death the deeds of the body, you will live.*
>
> *—Romans 8:12-13*

Some of you today belong to Jesus, but are struggling with a sin that just keeps coming back. Let me be clear—the flesh must be put to death. You must make the determination that through the power of the Holy Spirit you are going to crucify that sin. Jesus has made this possible, but it is your responsibility to put it to death. Don't live another day entangled in sin. Allow the Holy Spirit to give you the strength to put it to death. He will help you make the right decision and choose to follow Him to a joyful, glorious end!

Day 22

- -

PUTTING ON GRACE CLOTHES

- -

Therefore, as the elect of God, holy and beloved, put on tender mercies, kindness, humility, meekness, longsuffering;...

—*Colossians 3:12*

In yesterday's verses (Colossians 3:5-7), Paul instructed us on the things that we are to put to death and no longer practice, but now we get to the things we should be putting on, as disciples of Jesus.

It was William Barclay who said, "When a man becomes a Christian, there ought to be a complete change in his personality." And it was Warren Wiersbe who, in reference to the passages in Colossians chapter 3, spoke of "taking off the *grave* clothes and putting on the *grace* clothes."

Much like a piece of clothing, we are to remove those things that promote or build up our flesh and stifle our spiritual growth, and then we are to put on those things that build up our spirit and encourage the growth of the *new man*. Don't think this is a self-help program, because it is not. Both the removing of the old man and the putting on of the new man are results of being born again and allowing the Holy Spirit to do what He wants to do in your life, which is to make you into a man or woman of God.

Day 23

- -

FORGIVENESS AND HEALING

- -

...bearing with one another, and forgiving one another,
if anyone has a complaint against another; even as
Christ forgave you, so you also must do.

—Colossians 3:13

If you are "bearing with" someone, that person is affecting your life right now. I wonder if there is someone, or a number of people, with whom you are struggling right now? It may be a family member or a co-worker, and that old nature of yours is getting frustrated with them; you are tired of bearing with them. But the new nature says that you are to love them, and we know from 1 Corinthians 13 that love bears all things, hopes all things, believes all things, and endures all things. How can we possibly respond in love when our old nature is telling us that we've done enough, that to respond in love isn't worth the effort? Simple. God's Word shows us that as we walk in the Spirit, our old nature is put to death; the nature of Jesus will respond instead, and that response will be one of love.

Paul also instructs us here that as Jesus Christ has forgiven us, so are we to forgive others. Forgiveness involves dealing with things that have already happened. I know from talking with people over the years that there are many people who struggle with things from their past. They still remember things that their parents said or did. Hurts from an old boyfriend or girlfriend still affect them. And with so many of the stories I have heard, there is often a justifiable reason to assign blame. But we know from Scripture that Jesus forgives us completely—our sins have been erased by the blood of Jesus, never to be brought up again. Today, let us use Christ as our example, and forgive in the same way.

Day 24

- -

THANKFULNESS

- -

But above all these things put on love, which is the bond of perfection. And let the peace of God rule in your hearts, to which also you were called in one body; and be thankful.

—Colossians 3:14-15

Love and peace are two things that only the Holy Spirit can manufacture in us. Apart from this amazing work of God's Spirit, we cannot love with God's love, or experience the peace that passes all understanding that can rule in our heart. Yet as disciples of Jesus, we have the wonderful privilege to walk in God's love and experience God's peace. We should be very thankful!

Let me ask you; are you thankful for the air that is in your lungs today? Are you thankful for your spouse, your children, and your friendships? Are you thankful for the clothes on your back and the food in your cupboard? I know some of you are going through some pretty heavy trials right now, yet being thankful that God has counted you worthy and will give you the grace to handle every bit of pain and suffering that has come your way. Be thankful for those things that you see as setbacks, knowing that God has promised in Romans 8:28:

> *And we know that all things work together for good to those who love God, to those who are called according to His purpose.*

Now that you've read the passage from Romans, say it out loud. If you want to, say it again!

God will never allow you to go through more than you can handle, as it says in 1 Corinthians 10:13:

> *No temptation has overtaken you except such as is common to man; but God is faithful, who will not allow you to be tempted beyond what you are able, but with the temptation will also make the way of escape, that you may be able to bear it.*

He will actually, by His Spirit, work through all of these things to make you into a person of Christ-like character.

Day 25

THE WORD THAT DWELLS

---

*Let the word of Christ dwell in you richly in all
wisdom, teaching and admonishing one another in
psalms and hymns and spiritual songs, singing with
grace in your hearts to the Lord.*

—Colossians 3:16

This verse is really amazing. I believe Paul is telling us three very important things about God's Word.

First, it should dwell in us. To *dwell* means, "to live, to house, and to abide in." God desires His Word to live in us! These aren't just words of man that when we listen, it goes in one ear and out the other. No, this is God's Holy Word to us, and the words and passages should take root in your heart and live there.

Second, God's Word is able to give us wisdom, instruction, and the compassionate power to encourage and admonish those around us. You see, if these Words are truly dwelling (living) in you, then when circumstances arise you will be able to tap into those powerful words that will teach you and give you wisdom. The natural result will be to share the teachings with others.

Third, Paul tells us that one powerful way that God's Word dwells, roots itself, and lives in us is through music and singing. Praise, singing, and worship are very important in your life. Singing and praising God is a way to get God's words deep into your heart. I know that in my life, worship and singing praises to God have been such a powerful way that God's Word blesses and encourages me. When life throws a curveball at you, many times He brings a song into your heart that is so encouraging and uplifting.

So, allow the very words of Jesus to live in you, knowing that they will teach you and give you wisdom. We can rejoice with the psalmist when he says:

> *Therefore my heart greatly rejoices, and with my song I will praise Him!*
>
> —*Psalm 28. 7b*

Day 26

CHRIST-LIKE CHARACTER

And whatever you do in word or in deed, do all in the name of the Lord Jesus, giving thanks to God the Father through Him.

—*Colossians 3:17*

This verse is a wonderful conclusion to Paul's statements about seeking and setting our minds on the things above from Colossians 3:1-2 and "putting on" the wonderful Christ-like qualities from Colossians 3:12-16.

It's also a beautiful introduction to Paul's topic in Colossians 3:18-22 about our responsibilities as husbands and wives, fathers and mothers, and our relationships between employees and employers.

You see, it does not matter who you are, or what your social or occupational status is. Being raised with Christ means that we all have the awesome task of simply going about our day with Jesus in mind as our guide and decision-maker. Not *our* agendas, and not *our* plans. *His* plans. Paul says in today's Scripture, "*whatever* you do..." That pretty much sums it up, right? *Whatever* we set our minds on, make sure we think, perceive, and observe the way Jesus does. *Whatever* we set our hands on, make sure we do what Jesus wants us to do. And *whatever* we talk about with our friends or co-workers, make sure we say what Jesus wants us to say.

And all of this is done with a grateful and thankful heart. We don't say or do anything to earn our salvation or appease God. No, we have been raised with Christ! So the things we say and do are out of a thankful heart. We want to live a life out of thankfulness and gratitude for what He has done for us; His love shown on the cross and all of His blessings.

Day 27

- -

SERVING THE LORD HEARTILY

- -

And whatever you do, do it heartily, as to the Lord
and not to men, knowing that from the Lord you will
receive the reward of the inheritance; for you serve
the Lord Christ. But he who does wrong will be repaid
for the wrong which he has done, and there is no
partiality.

—Colossians 3:23-25

When you do something, anything, whatever you do, whether it be at work, home, church, a neighbors, do the very best you can. Treat anything you touch as a gift from God. He's given you the talents to do many things, so pour your joyful heart out into a task and go the extra mile to do a better job than expected, and dedicate it all to the Lord.

His promise to you is that He will reward you; you will receive the reward of the inheritance. The inheritance from your Heavenly Father is abundantly much more than you could ask or think. He owns the cattle on a thousand hills. He will send you so many blessings that your arms will not be able to contain them.

Have you ever volunteered for a ministry because it seemed like they could use your help? It seemed like something was giving you the confidence and inspiration to get involved and to give of your time and talents. That is the Lord, speaking in His still, small voice. He wants you to serve because He wants to bless you. And, when you got involved, you realized that it was a joy; you felt like you belonged. It was better than expected! That is the Lord confirming and blessing your answer to His call.

He has so many ways to bless us. He has all the riches and all of the love that any father could ever have. Take part in His inheritance. You cannot out-give Him. He will forever be the most generous Master of all.

And, conversely, if you do not do what is right in His sight, you will receive what is due for the wrong that you have done, no matter who you are—President, pastor, or pauper. He is God.

Day 28

CONTINUOUS, THANKFUL PRAYERS

Continue earnestly in prayer, being vigilant in it with thanksgiving.

—Colossians 4:2

To you, is prayer something you do before meals and when you go to bed? Or is it something, as Paul describes here, you do continually? Over the years of walking with Jesus, I have learned that prayer is simply a conversation with the glorious God of Heaven, and I don't want to do anything that would break that communication line.

Not only do I want to keep that communication line open, I want that communication to be from my heart. All throughout our home, Sandy and I have pictures of our children and grandchildren. And as I walk into a room, I will look at one of my granddaughters and just begin to pray, "Lord, keep her pure. Lord, make her into the woman you want her to be. Lord, prepare the heart of the little boy who will one day marry my little granddaughter."

Those are not just words that come out of my mouth from ritual or obligation. They flow right from my heart, and there is earnestness to them; a great deal of heart and effort is behind each of my prayers.

Like Paul, let me encourage you to *continue* in prayer; never stop. Don't break that communication with your Heavenly Father. Stay earnest and vigilant and you will see God do amazing things through those prayers.

Day 29

GRACIOUS WITNESS

Walk in wisdom toward those who are outside,
redeeming the time. Let your speech always be with
grace, seasoned with salt, that you may know how you
ought to answer each one.

—*Colossians 4:5-6*

As Christians, we are to be honest and upright in our dealings with people both in and outside of the church. We have the opportunity of pointing people to Jesus not only with our words, but also by our conduct. That is why Paul encourages us to redeem the time. We encounter many people only once in our lifetime, whether in the workplace, at the store, or in a park. Therefore, it is important to understand that we are privileged to be a witness for Jesus; perhaps the one and only witness that person will ever hear or see.

Now if you were to spend some time with me, it wouldn't take you too long to see some of the flaws that I have, just as I imagine I could see some flaws in you. But if I let my speech always be with grace, I will not want to point out any flaws. On the contrary, I will be saying things that build you up, encouraging you in your walk with Jesus, and trying to bring out the best in you. As our words are seasoned with salt, we will have the joy of adding some flavor to the lives of those around us by being agents of healing used by God, and the privilege of ultimately seeing someone come into a relationship with Jesus Christ. And notice that Paul says that our speech should *always* be full of grace, but only *seasoned* with salt. So, make sure you're spending more time giving out graceful words and carefully choosing those Godly salty words when necessary.

By our speech and our conduct we have the opportunity to bring joy or sorrow, give hope or discouragement, bring healing or pain. How are you going to redeem the time for the rest of your day?

Day 30

FULFILL YOUR MINISTRY

And say to Archippus, "Take heed to the ministry which you have received in the Lord, that you may fulfill it."

—Colossians 4:17

There are two great terms that Paul uses to conclude the book of Colossians that we should apply to our own lives: *take heed* and *fulfill*. First, Paul told Archippus to *take heed* to the ministry that he was given. Now, ministry here simply means *service* to God and His people. Surely, this is the responsibility of all Christians: to serve our Lord and one another. And we are to *take heed* of serving.

The Greek word for *take heed* means "to see to it" or "to pay close attention to it." Paul is asking that we not forget about serving God and His people. He wants us to continually see to it that we are serving one another. What a great encouragement to us today: let us never forget to be in an attitude of service.

Second, when we *see to* and *pay close attention to* serving one another, we are *fulfilling* that work of the ministry. You see, there's nothing else! The word *fulfill* literally means "to complete or bring to its whole." By serving one another, we are actually bringing to completion His tasks, and we are making the ministry whole. Yes, all of us together as a body, serving Him and serving one another, fulfills His ministry.

Let's be a people recognized by fulfilling the service that He has for us, and may He give us the strength to accomplish it.

You might also like...

- -

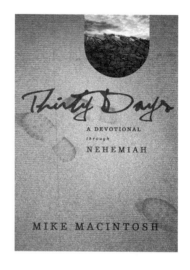

THIRTY DAYS
A DEVOTIONAL THROUGH NEHEMIAH
MIKE MACINTOSH
$9.99

ISBN-13: 978-160412-010-3

EXTRAVAGANT LOVE
AUDIO CD/MP3
MIKE MACINTOSH
$4.99

ISBN-13: 978-160412-003-5

NEED TOOLS TO HELP YOU GROW

Books

 Authors

 Multimedia

 Music

N YOUR FAITH?  Downloads

HORIZON**STORE**

www.myhorizonstore.com